GARY JONES

The Azores Islands

First edition

This book was professionally typeset on Reedsy.
Find out more at reedsy.com

Contents

Introduction

Now, you will be taken on a journey to the Azores Islands.

Officially called the Autonomous Region of the Azores, Portugal's Azores Islands is home to nine majestic volcanic islands. The islands are situated northeast of Brazil, east of New York City, southeast to Cape Verde and Newfoundland, and northwest of Madeira, giving them that unique, naturally beautiful vibe.

Sometimes called "The Other Eden", the Azores Islands truly is a paradise on its own—and of those serene havens you could ever set foot on. With emerald green lakes, lush vegetation, and sapphire skies, regal manor houses, and 15th century churches, amongst other beautiful things, it's no wonder that visitors get to fall in love with the islands, and always wish to come back. The islands also prove to be a great escape from the hustle and bustle of the city.

Given that there are nine incredibly beautiful islands, you will realize that you really have a lot to do while there—and you might get to learn more about their culture and dialect, too, since the locals are quite friendly and accommodating.

Read this book, and surely, after—or even while doing so—you will start planning your trip to the Azores already.

Once again, thank you, and enjoy.

1

Brief History and Background

The history of Azores Islands dates back to over 2,000 years, as seen in hypogea—carved earthen structures on rocks believed to be used for burials that were found on the Islands by Nuno Ribeiro, an archaeologist. What's interesting is that up until this day and age, it is still not known whether those carved structures were man-made or natural, but the truth remains that they predate the colonization of the Azores in the 15th Century.

The Catalan Atlas, an early map of the 13th to 14th centuries, showed that the islands were already around. There is also much controversy about who really discovered the Azores—from Golcaho Velco of the Henry the Navigator Ship, or the Berg of Bruges, Joshua Vander, who was a Fleming, and who supposedly landed in the Archipelago—specifically in the island of Santa Maria–while he was on his way to Lisbon—due to a storm. From then on, the Portuguese leaders learned about the islands, and named them after the Açor, also known as the Goshaw—although the said bird did not really live in the Islands. According to some sources, the Portuguese named them as such because of the fact that there's something about the islands that felt freeing—like you could find peace, and have time to enjoy while there.

The Portuguese settlers then started to develop the islands, first by clearing bush, and letting sheep loose on the island. The problem, though, was that other Portuguese did not want to reside on the islands for fear that they would have nothing to eat, and would have no means of living. So, what happened was that domesticated animals, such as pigs, goats, sheep, cattle, rabbits, and chickens were brought to live on the islands, and crops like sugar cane, grape vines, and other kinds of grains—and thus, people started living there, with the most number of settlers supposedly arriving back in 1444. These settlers originally came from Estremadura, Algarve, and Alto Alentejo.

In 1522, the original capital of the island, Villa Franca de Campo, was devastated by an earthquake—killing over 5,000 settlers. Over time, the island was rebuilt—and is now a yachting and fishing port.

In the 15th Century, brandy, wine, and barley, among other local goods, started to be exported to other places in the world.Later the islands were also able to survive the Liberal Wars. (Portuguese Civil War 1823 -1834)

In the 20th Century, Antonio de Oliviera Salazar, then the Portuguese ruler, was able to lease naval and air bases to the British Empire, as their contribution in the Second World War, and in 1945, a new air base was established at Lajes Field in Terceira Island, which now makes way for chartered and commercial flights in the Azores, as well as in North America, Africa, and Europe.

Finally, the Azores Islands reached autonomous status, and became the Autonomous Region of the Azores in 1976—and is now a prime destination for tourists and locals alike.

2

Weather and Best Times to Visit

While it is a collection of Islands, full sunny holidays may not be possible
in the Azores because rain and cloudy weather are always a possibility at
any time of the year, although the months April to May, and September
to October, in some years, prove to have higher temperature and longer

amounts of sunshine than the other months.

November to March

These months offer days that are bright and sunny, with some windy and wet days in between, and some cloudy and overcast days on the others.

Average temperature in these months is 11 to 17 C.

April to May

Bright sunshine and warm weather could be expected during these months.

Average temperature in these months is 11 to 24 C.

June to August

During these months, you'd be able to enjoy summer days that are warm and sunny. In areas where vegetation is present or in the west, it might be quite humid.

Average temperature in these months is 15 to 26 C.

September to October

Just like April to May, bright sunshine and warm weather could be expected during these months.

Average temperature in these months is 11 to 24 C.

When is it best to travel to the Azores?

It's best to avoid November to March as those are the winter months, and you might not be able to do much if you choose to go during those months.

Traveling between April and September, though, especially June to September would be great because of the sunny weather—and because then, you will be able to enjoy outdoor activities in the Azores.

3

Transportation to the Islands and Within the Islands

So, how exactly can you go to, and around Azores Islands? Read this chapter, and find out.

Getting to the Azores

You can fly to the Azores by taking any of the following airlines from Portugal or other European countries.

SATA Air Azores +351 296 209 720

This airline is headquartered at Ponta Delgada (São Miguel Island), and is the same one that's used to fly around all the islands of the Azores.

TAP Portugal +1 800-221-7370 | +1 973-624-6363

Headquartered at the Lisbon Portela Airport, this is Portugal's flag-carrier, and is one of the most trusted airlines in all of Europe.

TUI Airlines Netherlands +32 2 717 84 56

Once known as ArkeFly, this is a Dutch Charter airline that's situated at the Amsterdam Airport in Netherlands, with the TUI Group as its parent organization.

Ryan Air – 0871 246 0000 (UK)

If you are flying from the UK there are flights from Manchester and London to Ponta Delgada(São Miguel) with Ryan Air.

Getting Around

Meanwhile, if you're already there, here's what you can do to get around:

By Air

All of the islands work under the same airways, specifically SATA Air Azores, offering scheduled flights around the archipelago.

Just like buses, SATA Airplanes go from point to point every 20 minutes, and would then fly off to another island, and so on. This way, you will have no problems when it comes to island-hopping and seeing what the Azores have to offer.

SATA Air Azores

info@sata.pt
  (+351) 296 209 720

Car Rental

However, if flying by air is just not your thing, you may want to hire a car that you can drive around the islands, if that's what you desire. You can choose from people carriers or minis, but do take note that this service is relatively new to the islands, so make sure that you are careful, and be aware of signs posted on roads to avoid accidents and mishaps.

Also, take note that when hiring automobiles, you need to have a European style license—one with your photo on the left side. However, you can also use old-style licenses or passports, as long as you have them.

You can try these car rental companies below:

Santa Maria

Europcar Vila Do Porto
Aeroporto Santa Maria, 9580-908 Vila do Porto, Portugal

+351 296 886 528

Alvis Aluguer de Carros Santa Maria
9580-527 Vila Do Porto, Portugal

+ 351 296 886 528

Ilha Verde Rent a Car

Aeroporto de Santa Maria, 9580-908 Vila do Porto, Portugal

+351 296 886 528

Flores

Sixt Rent a Car

Santa Cruz Airport,Flores

+351 800 201 201

Magic Islands Rent a Car Santa Cruz das Flores

Santa Cruz Airport,Flores

+351 912 261 378

Terceira

Europcar Angra Heroismo Airport
Aeroporto Angra Heroismo Lages-Praia Da Vitoria,
Angra do Heroísmo

+351 295 513 722

AngraCar Rent
Às Pedreiras, 9700-251 Lajes, Portugal

+351 912 535 449

Graciosa

Rent-a-car Graciosa

+351 295 712 274
  +351 967 869 218
  +351 910 640 585

Sao Jorge

AzoreanWay Rent-a-Car
Largo Dr. João Pereira, 9800-527 Velas, Portugal

+351 912 533 239
  +351 295 098 343

reservas@azoreanwayrentacar.com

GREEN ISLAND Rent a Car
  Aeródromo de São Jorge Fajã da Queimada, Santo Amaro,Velas

+351 295 432 141

Pico Island

GREEN ISLAND Rent a Car
  Rua do Cachorro, Bandeiras, Pico - Açores, Madalena

+351 296 622 002

PicoWay Rent a Car
  Canada da Igreja, 9950-232 Criação Velha

+351 919 389 484

Faial Island

Ilha Verde Rent a Car
Castelo Branco HRT, 9900-321 Horta, Portugal

+351 292 943 945

Sixt Rent a Car
R. das Angústias nº 70 r/c, 9900-039 Horta, Portugal

+351 255 788 199

Sao Miguel

Rent-a-car Auto-ramalhense

Rua Direita Do Ramalho 158 A, Ponta Delgada – São Miguel

+351 296 281 104

GREEN ISLAND Rent a Car

Aeroporto João Paulo II, 9504-749 Ponta Delgada

+351 296 684 360

Ferries

You can also go around the islands by riding ferries that will allow you to sail between the islands of Flores and Corvo, Faila, Pico, and San Jorge, and also Sao Miguel and Santa Maria.

What you have to keep in mind, though, is that they do not operate 24/7, 365 days a year.

Atlanticoline Ferry

Rua Conselheiro Miguel da Silveira,Horta, Azores

comercial@atlanticoline.pt

+351 707 201 572

+351 292 200 381

Bus

There are buses traversing the islands all times of the year, and is probably the best alternative for flying by air. They are quite inexpensive, but the only problem is that they make take bits of your time as they are somewhat slow—and are mostly used by locals, rather than visitors.

However, if you really feel like riding a bus, you can try the following companies:

Caetano, Raposo E Pereira | +351 296 304 260

Auto Viacao Micaelense | +351 296 301 358
  transportes.avm@mercedes-benz.pt| transportes.avm@mercedes-benz.pt

Varela e Companhia, LDA | +351 296 301 800
  bensaude@bensaude.pt

Taxis

And of course, there are also taxis going around the islands that you can ride in. Just like ferries, they're also relatively new, but the great thing is that they have high standards—so you can expect only the best services around.

Now that you know how to get around, it's time to know what you can do, and where you can stay in all of the 9 islands. Read on, and find out.

4

Corvo Island

Corvo Island, also known as the Island of the Crow, is the northernmost and smallest island in the Azores Archipelago. It houses the pyroclastic tuff cones of the island's formative volcanic structures, and is cut by fault from the upper complexes of the archipelago. Sheer cliffs and coastal areas are also prevalent around here, and humidity reaches 85% in June.

Corvo is the smallest island in the Azores family of islands.If you want to experience isolation in the Atlantic ocean and get away from things then go to Corvo Island.Corvo has one small main village and very small airport.Corvo is a great place for some time away from everything and get into nature.

Getting To Corvo

There are daily ferries from Flores Island. A boat trip will take about 40 minutes to Corvo from Flores.

Atlanticoline Ferry
   Rua Conselheiro Miguel da Silveira,Horta, Azores
   comercial@atlanticoline.pt

+351 707 201 572
   +351 292 200 381

Where to Stay

Joe & Vera's Vintage Place +351 914 112 097
   Rua da Matriz, 9980-020 Corvo, Portugal

This Guesthouse has a great reputation for being sparkling clean and comfortable.Rooms have comfortable beds,TV,desks,private bath-rooms and a patio.

The breakfast here is famous and so is the personalized service.

The Pirates' Nest +351 963 731 953
Vila Do Corvo, Portugal

The Pirates' nest provides budget accommodation with everything you need to make your stay comfortable on the island.You will have free wifi and room service.The private rooms has comfortable beds and a TV .The kitchen and bathrooms are shared spaces.This accommodation is a family business and will give you a warm homely experience on the island.

Guest House Comodoro +351 292 596 128
Caminho Do Areeiro - Ilha Do Corvocorvo, Corvo Island, Portugal

This is a modest, house-like residence that provides no-fuss services, and humble amenities to tourists—and is getting great reviews at that, too.

Restaurants

Caldeirão, Restaurante - Pastelaria +351 927 727 977
Aeródromo do Corvo

O Caldeirao offers fresh and homemade bistro-style dishes, such as burgers, sandwiches, and steak, served with corn on the cob, and an assortment of fruits and vegetables—perfect while enjoying the fresh air coming from the Azores seas.

Bars and Clubs

For night time fun and leisure, do check out:

BBC Caffe and Lounge +351 292 596 030
   Avenida Nova BBC, Corvo 9980-0390

A simple, lounge-type bar that offers great fries and burgers, and night time drinks.

Fun Activities on the Island

While there, don't forget to visit:

Corvo Windmills

One of the oldest windmills in the world, the Corvo Windmills have that classic Mediterranean charm in them—and are actually smaller than other European models, with triangular sails and domes that'll surely amaze you.

Caldeirao Lookout

Visit this 300 m deep crater—which others say will also help you see the 9 islands' outlines. Wow.

Centro do Interpretacao do Corvo + 351 292 596 051
pncorvo.ciac@azores.gov.pt

Known as Corvo's historically classified area, the Centro do Interpretacao do Corvo is where you can learn more about the environment, and about the island's specifications, as well.

Beaches

There are no proper beaches in Corvo, but there definitely are bodies of water, and there's also the famous Caldeirao, a Caldera that's filled by a shallow lake with small volcanic cones that you can pay homage to. It's best to see it just by the coast, and is also a great place to try diving or snorkeling—and see old Corvo architecture down the seas.

5

Flores Island

Next up is Flores Island, an unspoiled territory that'll definitely give you some serenity as you try to leave the hustle and bustle of life behind, even for just a while. The island may get the highest amount of rainfall in all of Azores, it has a great variety of lagoons, an amazing botanical garden, and Cliff-side waterfalls that'll definitely leave you in awe.

Where to Stay

Rest and relax at the hotels listed below:

Hotel Servi-Flor +351 292 592 453
Antigo Bairro dos Franceses, Santa Cruz das Flores

Boasting of laid-back rooms, and majestic mountain or ocean views, this hotel is located on the east of the Flores Island, near Corvo, and offers French traditional cuisine, regional dishes, and a relaxing setting—together with a seasonal pool.

INATEL Flores +351 292 590 420
Zona do Boqueirão,Santa Cruz das Flores

With a world-famous friendly staff, beautiful ocean views, and a cliff-side setting, this proves to be a relaxing place of stay for locals and tourists alike.

Aldeia de Cuada +351 292 590 040
Faja Grande, 9960-070 Lajes Das Flores

A serene place to stay in, with paradise-like settings in the background, lush vegetation, and mountain views, you'd definitely relax and feel like you're one with nature while around here.This hotel is a group of abandoned cottages that was transformed into a hotel village.Great place for a relaxing stay.

Museums/Galleries

If museums are your thing, be sure to check out:

Museu das Flores +351 292 592 159
   Rua do Boqueirao, Largo Misericórdia, Santa Cruz das Flores

The museum offers incredible videos and installations regarding Azores' thriving whale community—and why you need to learn about them.

Restaurants

Por do Sol +351292552075
   Fajazinha, Lajes das Flores

Situated in one of Azores' traditional stone houses, the Por do Sol Restaurant offers amazing traditional food—such as sweet yams and seaweed patties that'll give you a better idea of what Azores really is about.

Restaurante O Moleiro +351 292 542 432
   Zona Industrial do Boqueirao, Santa Cruz das Flores

This blue-toned restaurant has some of the best dishes in all of Azores. Lots of customers say that they had an amazing time here—and that you should not forget to try their delicious grilled wreckfish.

Restaurante Casa do Rei +351 292 593 262
   Rua Peixoto Pimentel / Monte, Lajes das Flores

With cozy atmosphere, great architecture, and good food, you'd surely have a good time eating at this traditional Azorean restaurant.

Restaurante Beira Mar +351 292593153
  Isola di Flores, Lajes das Flores

Located at one of Flores' seaports, there's an inviting, calm atmosphere that you can enjoy while eating here. The owners/hosts are quite friendly, too, so you'd definitely have a good time eating here.

Bars and Clubs

E'legal +351 914 511 209
  FV69+2M Santa Cruz Das Flores

A Restaurant/bar with a great view,awesome food and nice place to enjoy a bottle of wine.

Bar O'Trancador +351 913 891 767
  Lajes ,Das Flores

This is a busy place on the weekends but a good place for a cold beer and a sandwich.

Coffee

Lanchonete "Orquídea" +351 292 592 096
  R. Alm. Gago Coutinho, Santa Cruz das Flores

Lanchonete "Orquídea" serves nice sandwiches,hamburgers, and tasty desserts.Good food and reasonable prices.

Lucino's Bar +351 292 592 633

Das Flores R. 25 de Abril,Santa Cruz das Flores

Cosy spot with nice sandwiches,burgers snacks and coffee.Lucino's Bar has a great terrace with a nice view.

Fun Activities on the Island

While there, don't forget to do the following:

Beaches

There are no "beaches" in Flores, but what you can do is enjoy the natural pools at Santa Cruz.

Go Scuba Diving

Discover what Flores has to offer by checking their amazing scuba-diving sites—all in crystal clear waters that'll help you define what Azores is all about.

Flores Dive Center
  Rua das Courelas, 9960-030 Fajã Grande
  +351 964 794 943

Try Hiking

Hike in the famous Azores trails and see various flora and fauna that you probably won't see anywhere else. Try WestCanyon Turismo Aventura for adventures around Flores.

WestCanyon Turismo Aventura
Rua do areeiro, número 52, Fazenda, 9970-243 Santa Cruz das Flores
Email: info@westcanyon.pt
+351 968266206

Poca da Alagoinha

Poço da Alagoinha

One of the most beautiful spots on the island is the magnificent waterfalls and lagoon Poço da Alagoinha.You will find this waterfall close to the village Fajazinha.

Lagoa Negra and Lagoa Comprida

Lagoa Negra and Lagoa Comprida are two amazing lakes with different colors.You will find these lakes up in the highlands area of Flores.

6

Faial Island

A trip to Azores would not be complete without visiting Faial Island—also known as the whale island because it's where you can
lookout for whales and appreciate what the seas have to offer.

With the wind in your hair, you might see the majestic sperm whale eat freshly-caught limpets, and see the famous Scrimshaw Museum, among others. Diving might be fun here, too.

Where to Stay

Here's where you can rest and relax at the island.

Faial Resort Hotel +351 292 207 400
   Rua Consul Dabney, 9901-856 Horta, Portugal

This resort is located near the Faial Marina. Surely, you'll be able to relax for the hotel offers ocean views, free Wi-Fi access, seasonal swim-up bars, and on-site restaurants that offer incredibly delicious dishes. Jacuzzi and Hammam are available, too.

Pousada Forte Horta +351 21 040 7670
Rua Vasco da Gama, 9900-017 Horta

Just a couple minutes away from the Botanical Gardens of Faial, this hotel is situated in a beautiful, 16th century fortress that provides amazing ocean and mountain views, and suites with separate living areas. Breakfast is available, as well.

Hotel do Canal Horta +351 292 202 120
Largo Dr. Manuel de Arriaga, 9900-026 Horta

What's amazing about this hotel is that it is tree-fronted and is near the ferry terminals, so you'll have plenty of opportunities to go around. The rooms are in subdued themes that will keep you warm and relaxed, and also get to enjoy a free buffet breakfast—alongside the free Wi-Fi access, of course.

Hotel Horta +351 292 208 200
R. Marcelino Lima, 9900-122 Horta

Near the mountains and the botanical garden, and a short walk from the Marina, Hotel Horta is one of the best budget hotels around, providing tourists with streamlined rooms. An outdoor pool is also around for your enjoyment.

Museums/Galleries

Museu da Horta +351 292 392 784
   Palácio do Colégio Largo Duque d' Ávila e Bolama, Horta

Located in one of Faial's most incredible buildings—Jesuit's College—this museum houses important parts of Azores' architecture and cultural heritage, with works by Mario Cesariny, Antonio Dacosta, and Sousa Pinto, amongst other people—and enjoy a walk along a white fig-tree lined pathway that'll give you time to relax and enjoy your trip more.

Museu do Scrimshaw +351 292 292 327
   Peter Café Sport Angustias 027, R. José Azevedo,Horta

The Museu do Scrimshaw is one of the best museums in the Azores, mostly because it holds a collection of various kinds of whale relics—made by the island's very own fisherfolk.

Restaurants

Canto da Doca +351 292292444
Rua Nova, Horta, Faial Island

This contemporary European restaurant offers great steak, burgers, fish, and fries—in a casual, laidback seating that would just allow you to relax and enjoy while eating—and see the amazing views that Faial has to offer.

Restaurante Genuino +351 292701542
Areinha Velha, 9, Horta, Faial Island, Portugal

Located in one of Horta's most scenic spots, you can enjoy great pasta meals and fish dishes here. You'd especially like their abalone, and enjoy the company of the restaurant's gracious host, too.

Pizzaria California + 351 292392082
Rua Almeida Garrett #4, Horta, Faial Island 9900-075

If you're craving for pizza while at Faial Island, make sure to drop by this amazing Pizzeria that offers various kinds of authentic Italian pizza—with a Portuguese twist. Pizzas are freshly made, and the casual vibe of the restaurant would help you feel right at home.

Coffee Shops/Cafes

Casa Teahouse and Bar +351 292 700 053
  Rua de Sao Bento, Horta, Faial Island, Portugal

With majestic views of Azores' churches, and flowers and plants all around, you'd surely have a relaxing time having coffee or tea at this great little coffee shop. Don't forget to try their orange cake, and walk along the banana trees, too.

Café Volga +351 292 292 347
  Praça Infante Dom Henrique 16, 9900-016 Horta, Portugal

Very affordable and tasty food for after a long day at the beach.Burgers, sandwiches,fries and good coffee.It also has a daily set lunch menu.

Casa de Chá +351 292 700 053
　　Rua De São João 38 A, 9900-129 Ilha do Faial, Portugal

Great place for sandwiches and Salsa with some vegan and vegetarian options.Fresh food with a nice garden to relax and enjoy your meal.

Bars and Clubs

Peter's Café Sport +351 (0) 292 292 327
　　Rua Jose Azevedo "Peter", 9, Horta, Faial Island

Located near the famous Scrimshaw Museum, you can talk about sailing, sports, and other amazing things with locals at this bar.

Gastro bar Príncipe+351 967 173 184
　　Estrada Príncipe Alberto de Mónaco, 9900-050 Horta

This place is more a restaurant than a bar but it's a great place for a bottle of wine and good food.The gastro bar has a nice ambiance and friendly staff.

Fun Activities on the Island

While there, don't forget to do the following:

Go Whale Watching

With 20 different kinds of whales in the Azorean seas, you'd surely have a spectacular time trying to know this species—truly a magical, unforgettable sight to behold.

You can experience the whales by booking a tour with The Naturalist Tourism.They have experienced guides with lots of whale knowledge.

The Naturalist Tourism
   Phone: +351 968 327 633
   Largo Dr. Manuel de Arriaga, 9900-026 Horta

Go Horse Riding

Walk around Faial and you'll see Cruzado and Lusitano horses that you can rent to ride on—and see Faial in a whole new different light.

The Patio Horse & Lodge offers Horseback riding for beginners and experienced riders.

Patio Horse & Lodge
   Phone: +351 917 428 111

Visit the Faial Botanic Garden
   Phone: +351 292 948 140

The botanical gardens boast of orchards and old pastures, and is located at the Valley of Flamingos, specifically at the Sao Lorenco Farm—where you'd get to see flora and fauna of every kind.

Visit the Ponta Dos Capelinhos Lighthouse

While it has not been in use since 1957, the Lighthouse is still in-tact—and with it comes the history of Faial, after surviving a couple of volcanic eruptions.

Capelinhos Volcano

Capelinhos is a Monogenetic Volcano that is one of those places that you have to see.The views from the top of the mountain is worth the trek alone.The last time there was an eruption was in 1957 and you can clearly see the effects of that event.Many travelers say the place feels more like Mars than earth.

Capelinhos

You can book a volcano tour with Ourisland-Azores.

Ourisland-Azores
   (+351) 967 172 754

Go On A Jeep Tour

If you don't like hiking and climbing then taking a jeep tour might be more your thing.Book a jeep tour around the island and see the best of the island form the comfort of a jeep.You can book a tour with Azores Toboga.

Azores Toboga
   + 351 968 749 742
   azores@toboga.pt

Trekking

Faial has some fantastic trekking routes.You have the option to do half day or full day excursions.Endemic is a company that offers great treks and other special activities like surfing and farming.

Endemic Azores
  +351 918 191 180

Snorkelling And Scuba

Dive Azores has great packages for individuals or groups to experience the great diving spots on the island.The staff is friendly and helpful.There also offer beginner and advance dive training.

Dive Azores
  +351 96 788 22 14
  info@diveazores.net

Beaches

Beach of Porto Pim

This small beach is a great place to relax in the sun and do some snorkeling. This is a beach with a lifeguard, restrooms, and restaurants. So its a nice spot for a relaxing day at the beach.

Praia do Almoxarife

Praia do Almoxarife in Horta is a calm and beautiful beach. The grey sand and stunning views make it easy to spend hours on this lovely beach.

7

Graciosa Island

Graciosa is in the northernmost part of the central Azores Islands and houses a majestic and unforgettable volcanic cave that you definitely have to set foot on while there. Check out the island's basalt windmills and dwarf donkeys that may even help you see the island's famous whales.

This island is one of the more secluded islands and to be honest not my first choice to visit if you have a short time in the Azores.However if you have time and want to spend some time in a quiet and secluded island then come to Grociosa island.

Where to Stay

Graciosa Resort - Biosphere Island Hotel +351 295 730 500
Porto da Barra,Santa Cruz da Graciosa

Very nice 4 star hotel located just outside the city centre but its still close enough to walk to the more busy areas.Very clean and has comfortable beds.The staff is very helpful.

Residencial Ilha Graciosa Hotel +351 295 730 220
Av. Mouzinho de Albuquerque 49, Santa Cruz da Graciosa

Very cosy hotel with fast and reliable wifi.This hotel is a restored manor house and has a nice homely feel to it.It has a nice garden area for you to relax and take in the beautiful scenery.

Casa da Madrinha Graciosa +351 918 449 656
Fonte do Mato, no27,Tras dos Pomares

Another old house in Graciosa that has been beautifully renovated and transformed into a guesthouse.Rooms are private and some has ocean views.Great value for money and one of those places that you will find peaceful and relaxing.The rooms are private with a shared bathroom and free wifi.

Museums/Galleries

Museu da Graciosa +351 295 712 429
Lrg. Conde Simas, 17, Santa Cruz da Graciosa

This gorgeous museum is not just aesthetically beautiful, it'll also help you learn more about the history of Graciosa itself.

Restaurants

Restaurante Costa do Sol +351 295 712 694
Santa Cruz Da Graciosa

Great food,good service and a cozy atmosphere is what you get at Costa Do Sol.Try out the house burger you won't be disappointed.

Dolphin Snack Bar +351 295 712 014
9880-120 Carapacho, Portugal

This is a nice restaurant with a nice day buffet and tasty burgers. It also has a nice variety of tasty seafood dishes.This restaurant is simple and good value for money.The nice view from the restaurant is a bonus.

Restaurante Estrela do Mar +351 295 712 560
12, Porta da Folga, Portugal

Great place to eat some fresh fish and a nice salad.This place is simple and has a rustic feel to it .Also has a nice view over the bay.

Fun Activities on the Island

While there, don't forget to:

Go Yachting

Graciosa's oceans are crystal clear—so it would be a shame not to be able to experience it for what it is. Therefore, yachting really should be done, so you'd not only get to traverse the seas, you might see wondrous dolphins, too—and they'll accompany you to the crossings of the island. Amazing.

Calypso Yacht Charter

info@calypsoazores.com

+351 295 732 892

+351 917 566 500

See some whales.

Whale watching is also prevalent in Graciosa, and surely, you'll be amazed at how majestic the whales are.

Try hydro-thermal spas.

Graciosa has a bevy of hydro-thermal spas that you can enjoy, and will surely help you relax in iron water pools, and the beautiful waterfalls of Azores.

TERMAS DO CARAPACHO
  +351 295 714 212
  Rua Dr. Manuel de Menezes
  9880120 Carapacho
  Graciosa

Diving

Graciosa Island is a great place to dive for both beginners and more advanced divers.It's easy to find good spots to dive around the island but if you're going to spend a short time on the island then get a diving company to guide you. Contact Nautico Graciosa to help find the best spots.

Nautico Graciosa
  +351 295 732 811
  divingraciosa@sapo.pt
  Santa Cruz Da Graciosa, Portugal

Beach

Carapacho Natural Swimming Pools

There are no famous beaches on the island but you will have a great time swimming in the Carapacho Natural Swimming Pools.

8

Pico Island

Pico island is famous for its big mountain and spectacular ocean scenery.This volcanic island has a wide range of activities that will make your time on this island something to remember.

Where to Stay

L´ESCALE DE L´ATLANTIC +351 292 666 260
   Caminho do Morro N. 2, Calhau, 9930-214 Piedade

This homely and tranquil bed and breakfast hotel is a great choice to stay at while in Pico Island. The hotel has a warm and cosy feel to it with a big garden and great views. The rooms are very comfortable, and the breakfast is something you will remember.

Miradouro da Papalva Guest House Inn +351 965 392 280
   Ramal Salazar, nº13, São João

The wonderful and unique bed and breakfast will make your stay on the island one you will never forget: great location, beautiful views, great food and warm hospitality. You also get free wifi and a TV in your room. This is an excellent place for couples to stay at.

Epicenter PICO +351 913 170 613
   R. Dr. Manuel de Arriaga n.º 23,Madalena

In the Azores you will see a lot of nice views but the view at this home/guesthouse is outstanding. Great place to spend a weekend or longer and enjoy the unique view of Pico. The rooms come with wifi, phone, and airconditioning.

Aldeia Das Adegas +351 292 642 000
   GM9M+74 S.Roque do Pico

Classic looking exterior and modern interior apartments in a fantastic setting. The rooms are spotless and comfortable with free wifi and TV.The kitchen is fully equipped so you can do your own cooking while on the island.

Pocinho Bay +351 292 629 135
  Pocinho, 9950-154 Candelária

Beautiful place to stay with a view over the ocean. Nice swimming pool and great hospitality. The rooms are clean, modern and comfortable. This hotel has some special facilities like an outdoor shower and a hot tub.

Museums/Galleries

Museu dos Baleroois +351 292 679 340
  R. dos Baleeiros 13, 9930-143 Lajes Do Pico

Another whale exhibit-dedicated museum, you'll find that there's still lots to be learned about Pico's famous whales, and with the help of this museum, you will surely understand why.

Whaling Industry Museum +351 292 642 096
Rua do Poço 9940 - São Roque do Pico
museu.pico.info@azores.gov.pt

Learn about the importance of the whaling industry at the Whaling Industry Museum.

Pico Vineyard

Museu do Vinho +351 292 622 147 (Wine museum)
Rua do Carmo, Toledos 9950 – Madalena
museu.pico.info@azores.gov.pt | http://www.museus.azores.gov.pt/

Boasting of age-old dragon trees, distilleries, and a cellar, this museum has that old-school, rustic charm that'll definitely give you a piece of history—and help you learn more about the Azores while checking out the old Carmelite Conceptual House.

Restaurants

Restaurante A Parisiana +351 292 623 771
R. Alexandre Herculano 11, Madalena

If you are someone that enjoy buffets meals then this the place for you. Nice food and good service. This restaurant has a nice patio for drinks at the end of a long day on this lovely island.

Adega "A Buraca" +351 292 642 119
   Estrada Regional 1, 35 Santo António, Santo António

Nice Seafood dishes and some good wine.Lovely atmosphere and friendly staff.

Casa ncora +351 292 644 496
   Rua do Cais 29-B, São Roque do Pico

Great food with a different menu every day. So the dishes are limited, but the food is excellent. The place is well worth the visit and the views over the island is great.

Tasca "O Petisca" +351 292 622 357
   Avenida Padre Nunes da Rosa , Madalena

The cheese platter in this restaurant is famous, and so is the white sangria.Good atmosphere and good service.Very nice local food.

Madalena

Coffee Shops/Cafes

Caffe 5 + 351 292 623 970
Rua Carlos Dabney ,Madalena, Madalena, Pico

With a warm, comfortable ambience, you'd surely enjoy a warm cup of coffee, steak, and fries in this incredible little coffee house.

Esplanada DARK +351 912 361 025
9950-305 Madalena, Portugal

Perfect place for a light meal,beer or coffee.This is the type of place you go to take a break from walking around the island and just take in the atmosphere on the island.

Bars and Clubs

Café Concerto +351 292 623 842
  Caminho do Rosário, 45, 9950-233 Madalena do Pico, Portugal

Good place for drinks,beers and a relaxing afternoon or evening.Good music and good atmosphere.

Cella Bar +351 292 623 654
  Rua Da Barca, 9950-303 Madalena, Portugal

This place is kind of a touristy place to eat but It still a very good place to spend an afternoon or evening.I say this a lot of Azores but again this place has great views and excellent service. This restaurant might not be 'old school" Azores, but it has good food and excellent service.

Fun Activities on the Island

While there, don't forget to do the following:

Try Geotourism Activities

See, Azores has a history of being founded after 1766 volcanoes—so definitely, there's a lot of archaeological digs that could be done. With the help of UNESCO, you can take part in some of the island's many geotourism tours that'll help you understand the history of Azores, and of the volcanoes it came from, too, and surely, you'll get such a great tourist advancement that you have never experienced before.

Climbing Mount Pico

If you are a hiker or climber, then a day climb up Mount Pico might be the thing for you. Although Pico is not one of the highest mountains in the world, it is a challenging climb. That being said if you are in reasonable physical shape, then you would be able to climb it. Just make sure you bring your hiking boots and come prepared. The best way to to do it with a certified guide and Tripix Azores is one of those companies that will guide you up the mountain.

Tripix Azores
   Cais da Madalena Pico, 9950-305 Madalena, Portugal
   info@tripixazores.com
   +351 963 778 109
   +351 292 623 616

+351 912 087 199

Join Bike Tours. (Tripix)

Bike along Pico's trails and you'd realize how much of Azores there is to see—and why flora and fauna matter.

Tripix
  Cais da Madalena Pico, Madalena
  info@tripixazores.com
  +351 963 778 109
  +351 292 623 616

Whale Watching

Espaço Talassa, observation des baleines et dauphins(Azores whale Watching Base)

To experience the Whales, Dolphins and another sea wildlife book a tour with the Azores whale Watching Base. The guides are very knowledgeable and friendly. They have well-organized tours that put safety first.

Azores whale Watching Base
  9930-136 Lajes Do Pico
  +351 292 672 010

Kayak

Another fun way to really get into the action on Pico island is doing a guided Kayak tour. You can book a tour with Pico Island Adventures

Pico Island Adventures Kayak Tours

Rua Doutor Freitas Pimentel R/C, Madalena
+351 292 622 980

Beaches

There are loads of swimming holes on the island however not many sandy beaches.

Canto da Areia

This is the only beach on the island where you will find some sand. So if you want a sandy beach, then this is the spot to go to on Pico. It's not a big beach but its still a beautiful place with nice views.

Car or Scooter Rental

A great way to experience the beauty of Pico island is to rent a scooter. And if a scooter isn't your thing then rent a car a just drive around the island and find all the secluded spots around this magnificent island.

Pico Island Adventures Scooter Rental
  Rua Doutor Freitas Pimentel R/C, 9950-334 Madalena
  +351 292 622 980

9

Sao Jorge Island

Sao Jorge is known as one of the most dramatic islands in the Azores Archipelago, mostly because of its fjord-like lakes, and wave-lashed cliffs. With natural trails and lots of trees, there are always a lot of birds to see, fish to swim with, and whales to watch out for. They also have picturesque villages and vineyards that'll help you feel one with nature—and with the archipelago itself. This island is also the surfing capital of the Azores.

Where to Stay

Rest and relax at the hotels listed below:

Hospedaria Austrália +351 295 412 210
Rua Doutor Teófilo de Braga, Velas, São Jorge

Spacious rooms with a big living area and kitchen.Good value for money hotel with a great breakfast and good service.

Aldeia da Encosta +351 916 212 185
Rua dos Degraus, S/ nº, Velas – Ilha de São Jorge

This is a fantastic house rental. The house is clean and neat.The place has a beautiful bbq place outside on the terrace and the usual great Pico views. You also get comfortable beds and free wifi.The host is very helpful and friendly.

Quinta da Magnólia +351 295 414 211
  São Mateus Urzelina, Urzelina

This renovated old farmhouse is now a beautiful modern boutique hotel. This hotel has very comfortable beds and an incredible breakfast. The pool is fantastic, with stunning views over the ocean. This hotel comes highly recommended, and the service is something you will remember.

Restaurants

Restaurante Booka +351 911 834 425
  Avenida do Livramento, 9800-522 Velas São Jorge, Portugal

Great food, hospitality, and service.This cozy restaurant has excellent food at reasonable prices. The fish and meat menu is both really good.

A Quinta +351 295 432 590
  Faja de Santo Amaro 93, Velas

The customer service and staff make this place great. And the food makes it almost perfect. Very good restaurant and you can try something different from the menu every day and come back for more. This is one of the best restaurants in the Azores.

Restaurante Urzelina +351 295 414 016

Urzelina, São Jorge

This is the best all you can eat buffet restaurant on the island. And the buffet is not the only great thing. The whole menu is fantastic and the food is of high quality. Both seafood and meat are delicious. And as usual in the Azores, all this comes with a great view and location.

Bars and Clubs

Caffe Recanto +351 295 412 195
MQHR+R9 Velas, Portugal

Simple cafe for drinks and beer.No food is served here. Good place for a bit of music and drinks with friends.

Bar da Tertúlia +351 295 432 038
Pico da Caldeira Levadas, São Jorge, Velas

A simple bar to have a few drinks and eat light meals. Just a good place for a few drinks and a relaxing evening.

Fun Activities on the Island

While there, don't forget to do the following:

Go Bird Watching

Azores have a lot of bird species that you'd be in awe to see—these in-clude the storm petrels, the bullfinch, and the goldcrest, among others. Watch as the birds take flight and come home to their nests—and just be in awe of them living in such a beautiful natural reserve.

Try Fishing

Catch some fish—such as tuna and blue marlin, rig a boat, and just feel like you're part of the fishing community—even for once.

If you want to have a professional fishing experience in Sao Jorge then contact a company called Velasfishingtur. This company also do snorkeling tours around the island.

Velasfishingtur
   MQJW+27 Velas, Portugal
   +351 919 821 513

Try Boating

Sao Jorge has beautiful, pristine seas—so it would be a shame not to be able to experience it for what it is. Therefore, boating really should be done, so you not only get to traverse the seas, you might see wondrous dolphins, too—and they'll accompany you to the crossings of the island. Amazing.

Try out a sailing tour with The São Jorge Sail Center and get a unique perspective of the island with experienced sailors.

São Jorge Dive and Sail Center
   9800-527 Velas, Portugal
   +351 915 106 268

Go Scuba Diving

Discover what Sao Jorge has to offer by checking their amazing scuba-diving sites—all in crystal clear waters that'll help you define what Azores is all about.

If you want to have a unique diving experience then again I recommend São Jorge Dive and Sail Center. They offer diving courses for beginners and more advanced divers. This company is very professional and experienced.

São Jorge Dive and Sail Center
   9800-527 Velas, Portugal
   +351 915 106 268

Natural Swimming Pools

Go for a swim in the Natural Swimming Pools in Velas and experience the natural pools formed by ancient volcanic eruptions. There are facilities like showers, toilets, and even a bar. These swimming pools also have a lifeguard on duty to keep an eye on swimmers.

Beaches

Fajã da Caldeira

Fajã da Caldeira is the best beach on the island and is famous amongst the surfing community. There is even a surf camp guesthouse for people to enjoy everything this lovely beach has to offer.

Caldeira Guesthouse & Surfcamp
  Fajã da Caldeira, 9850-205 RIBEIRA SECA CHT, Portugal
  +351 912 517 001

Try Hiking

Hike in the famous Azores trails and see various flora and fauna that you probably won't see anywhere else.

For hiking, canyoning and kayaking try out the Discover Experience Azores. They will set you up to have an outdoor experience of a lifetime.

Discover Experience Azores
  Fajã dos Vimes, 9850-213 São Jorge Açores, Portugal
  +351 967 552 354

10

Sao Miguel

Sao Miguel is the biggest island in the Azores Archipelago—and is definitely one of the most unforgettable. It kind of gives you the feeling that you're able to see how the volcanic eruptions shaped Azores into what it is today.

It has that old-time, rustic charm that you probably want to see in such a majestic archipelago, with cobbled, mosaic streets, and geothermal heat. Gardens and seas are also around for you to enjoy, and you should check out the beautiful cicadas, too.

Where to Stay

Royal Garden Hotel +351 296 307 300
R. de Lisboa, Ponta Delgada - Açores, Portugal

With a subtle Japanese theme, this beautiful hotel has impeccable interiors, rooms with balconies, grand living areas, and free Wi-Fi access—all while you get amazing ocean or mountain views. The restaurant is also glass-sided for you to enjoy more.

Pedras do Mar Resort & SPA +351 296 249 300
Rua das Terças 3, Ponta Delgada

Pedras do Mar Resort & SPA is a nice 5 star hotel with a great location. It has a beautiful infinity pool with a stunning view of the ocean. The rooms come with views over the mountain or the ocean. You can sit on your balcony and take in the beautiful sights of Sao Miguel.

Santa Barbara Eco-Beach Resort +351 296 470 360
Morro de Baixo, Ribeira Grande, Portugal

This lovely Eco-Beach Resort is located on the northern coast of the island. This resort gives you direct access to the beach, swimming pool, and restaurant. All the villas are modern and created with sustainable material. All rooms have wi-fi, air conditioning, and TV.

The Lince Azores +351 296 630 000
   Av. Dom João III 29, Ponta Delgada

This 4-star hotel is located close to the Ponta Delgada Marina. The Lince Azores Hotel offers modern and comfortable rooms with mountain or sea views. Make some time to hang out at the beautiful outdoor pool and sauna.

Museums/Galleries

Furnas Monitoring and Research Center +351 296 206 745
   Rua da Lagoa das Furnas 1489, 9675-090 Furnas

This museum is an interpretative center that'll help you learn more about Sao Miguel and how it came to be. While here, you'd also get to learn more about why it's important to improve Azores' ecosystem, and why water supply has to be recuperated.

Museu Carlos Machado +351 296 202 930
Rua do Dr.Guilherme Poças 65, Ponta Delgada

Dr. Carlos Machado created this museum in 1876. The museum features collections on Natural History, African ethnography, and Regional ethnography.

Museu Casa do Arcano +351 296 473 339
Rua Joao d'Horta Matriz, Ribeira Grande, Sao Miguel

This museum is interesting for it used to be a nun's home—and while there, she created miniature biblical scenes—scenes that you can still see today. Learn about it, or learn her story by visiting this place.

Ponta Delgada

Restaurants

Taberna Açor +351 296 629 084
R. dos Mercadores 41, Ponta Delgada

This is an excellent traditional Portuguese restaurant with great food, atmosphere, and service. You might wait a bit for your food to arrive, but once it arrives, you will be glad you came here. So come for lunch or dinner, have few drinks and then wait for your amazing food. Taberna Açor is traditional Portuguese food at its best.

Restaurante da Associação Agrícola de São Miguel +351 296 490 001
Campo Do Santana, Recinto Da Feira Rabo de Peixe 37
Ribeira Grande

This is another great restaurant on the island with a wide variety of dishes. But if you like steak, then this is the restaurant to visit in Sao Miguel. The steaks here are on a different level. While you wait for the food, get one of their tasty cocktails, and enjoy the nice atmosphere and service.

Lagoa Azul +351 296 915 678
   R. da Caridade 28, Sete Cidades

In the mood for an all you can eat buffet? Then this is the place for you. Wide variety of Fish and Meat Dishes. Lagoa Azul is family cooked food with great service and excellent value for money.

Tony's Restaurant +351 296 584 290
   Largo do Teatro 5, Furnas

If you want to eat at Tony's then make a reservation because this place is very popular. The food at this restaurant is fantastic, and the service is excellent. Great variety of meat, fish, and cheeses.

Coffee Shops/Cafes

Café Royal +351 296284176
   Rua Alfandega 4/6, Ponta Delgada, Sao Miguel

Offering not just coffee, but also fresh seafood dishes, this is definitely one of the most unique coffee shops around the world.

Tea House " O POEJO" +351 296 915 674
da, R. Eça de Queiroz 203 , Rio Tinto

Beautiful tea house with a courtyard so you can sit outside and enjoy the view.The cafe has a nice variety of light meals, cakes, and cookies. Great spot for lunch or just a cup of tea or coffee.

Intz48 Coffee Roasters Azores +351 296 707 655
R. Hintze Ribeiro 46-48, Ponta Delgada

This cafe has the best coffee in the Azores. Beautiful place to enjoy light meals, coffee, and a slice of cake. The cafe has fast wifi and a cozy interior. Remember to try the cheesecake at Intz48; it is outstanding.

Bars and Clubs

Tojo Bar +351 296 473 405
Largo do Rosario Matriz, Ribeira Grande

Tojo Bar is the type of bar you get together with friends and relax. Play pool or Foosball and enjoy a fun evening with a cold beer.

Beach Bar & Grill +351 296 381 783
Estr. Regional do Pópulo 13, Ponta Delgada

Beach Bar & Grill the name tells you everything you need to know. Cold beer and good food right next to the ocean. The staff is friendly, and the prices are reasonable.

Dinu's Bar +351 918 626 020

Rua Ernesto do Canto nr 23,Ponta Delgada

Nice place to relax and have fun with friends as it offers scenic views of the city, together with amazing service from the staff.

Lava Jazz +351 917 350 418
  Avenida Roberto Ivens, 9500-239 Ponta Delgada

Live music ,nice drinks and excellent atmosphere.It all makes for a good night out in Ponta Delgada. The service is excellent, and the bar also serves light meals.

Fun Activities on the Island

While there, don't forget to do the following:

See some Whales

Whale watching is also prevalent in Sao Miguel, and surely, you'll be amazed at how majestic the whales are.Moby Dick Tours have organized tours to go see the whales, dolphins and other marine life. Their tours are professional and well organised.

Moby Dick Tours
Av. Infante Dom Henrique, Ponta Delgada, Portugal
E-mail: azoreswhale@gmail.com
Mobile: (+351) 919 942 831
Office: 296 583 643

Go Bird Watching

Azores has a lot of bird species that you will be in awe to see—these include the storm petrels, the bullfinch, and the goldcrest, amongst others. Watch as the birds take flight and come home to their nests—and just be in awe of them living in such a beautiful natural reserve.

Bio & Bird Tours have bird watching tours in all-terrain vehicles all over the island. Good way to see the birds with an experienced local.

Bio & Bird Tours
  São Miguel Açores
  info@bioandbird.com
  +351 914 027 828

Canyoning and Coasteering

If you are an adventurer at heart, then canyoning and coasteering is something you might be interested in while in the Azores. Azorean

Active Blueberry is an adventure company that organizes Canyoning and Coasteering events on Sao Miguel. The company is professional and places its customer's safety first.

Azorean Active Blueberry
info@azoreanactiveblueberry.com
+351 914 822 682

Kayaking

Kayaking is one of the best ways to experience the beauty of Sao Miguel. It gives you a unique perspective and places you very close to the ocean and the marine life of the Azores. You can contact the adventure company Fun Activities Azores Adventure to go on a kayak adventure.

Fun Activities Azores Adventure
info@fun-activities.net
+351 911 014 212
+351 967 451 256

Try Hiking

Hike in the famous Azores trails and see various flora and fauna that you probably won't see anywhere else.Contact Fun Activities Azores Adventure for more information.

Fun Activities Azores Adventure
   info@fun-activities.net
   +351 911 014 212
   +351 967 451 256

Try Fishing

Catch some fish—such as tuna and blue marlin, rig a boat, and just feel like you're part of the fishing community—even for once.To go a fishing trip contact the Azores Fishing Center.

Azores Fishing Center

Av. Infante Dom Henrique, Ponta Delgada

+351 914 426 347

+351 914426

info@azoresfishingcenter.com

booking@azoresfishingcenter.com

Rest and relax in a fun way

Spas

Sao Miguel has a bevy of hydro-thermal spas that you can enjoy, and will surely help you relax in iron water pools, and the beautiful waterfalls of Azores. Make sure to take a hot spring bath at the Termas de Ferraria, too.

TERMAS DA FERRARIA
Rua Ilha Sabrina,Edifício Termas da Ferraria, GINETES Island ,São Miguel
Email- termasdaferraria@gmail.com
+351 296 295 669

Beaches

Sao Miguel has a lot of beaches that can even be accessed from other parts of the archipelago, given that it is the biggest, and are found near most hotels. Moisteros may prove to be the best one, or just check out the whole line of Sao Miguel Azores Beaches.

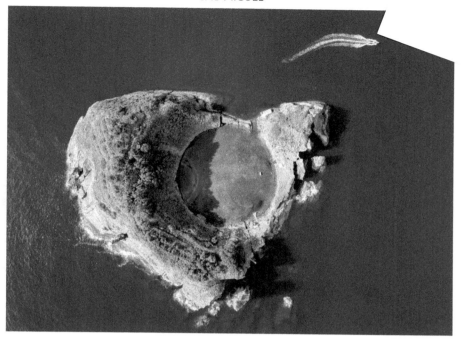

Islet of Vila Franca do Campo

This little island just of the coast of São Miguel is a must-see while in the Azores. If you like swimming, sunbathing, snorkeling and other ocean activities then spend a day on the Islet of Vila Franca do Campo. I suggest going early to get a boat from the harbor before it gest crowded. It's a quick 5 min boat trip but you want to spend the whole day on the island.

For information and Tickets to Islet of Vila Franca do Campo :
    +351 911 927 039
    +351 295 539 100
    bilheteira@cnvfc.net

Praia de Santa Barbara
    Ilha de São Miguel, Ribeira Grande

A beautiful and unique beach with black volcanic sand. The black sand and blue water is something different and creates, and an atmosphere you get nowhere else. Get a beer at the beach cafe and relax. If you are into surfing, then you will enjoy Praia de Santa Barbara.

Information: +351 296 470 730

Mosteiros Beach

São Miguel, R. da Areia 40, Mosteiros, Portugal

On the western coast of the island, you will find this beautiful black volcanic sand beach. One of the best feautures of this beach is the significant black rock formations standing out of the water.

Agua D' Alto Beach

Água D'Alto Beach

Água D'Alto is a beautiful open sandy beach and great for a day with the family. If you want a beach with no rocks and more sand, then this is the spot for you Great beach for swimming.

11

Santa Maria Island

Santa Maria was the very first island that came out of those volcanic eruptions all those centuries ago, and that is why it holds a very special place in the hearts of the people of Azores.Santa Maria has a fascinating history and was home to an allied airbase in World War II.

But aside from its history, Santa Maria has definitely a lot to offer—with various birds in flight, basalt columns, pale yet beautiful sand, and warm weather that tourists definitely like. While there, you can try kayaking or jet-surfing, check the whales, and walk beautiful trails that'll help you admire the Azores more.

Where to Stay

Hotel Colombo +351 296 820 200
   Rua Alto da Cruz 473, 9580-473 Vila do Porto, Portugal

This 4-star hotel is located as you drive into the city Vila do Porto. The hotel swimming pool is fantastic with a great view of the ocean and a deck bar for your convenience.

Hotel Santa Maria - Açores +351 296 820 660
   Rua da Horta Vila do Porto, Vila do Porto

Wonderful 4 star hotel with a big garden and friendly staff. The hotel is located close to the airport and the city area. The rooms are big and very clean. The hotel has a big swimming pool, and the breakfast is excellent.

Charming Blue +351 296 883 560
   Rua Teófilo Braga 31, Vila do Porto

Charming Blue is a very comfortable 3-star hotel located in Vila do Porto. The food and service at this hotel are outstanding. Very relaxing hotel with a lovely pool area. The rooms are comfortable and spacious.

Restaurants

Mesa d'Oito +351 296 882 083
Rua Teófilo de Braga nº1, Vila do Porto

This restaurant is located in the Charming blue hotel.Good service and good food at reasonable prices.

Clube Naval Bar / Restaurante +351 296 883 058
Marina de Leça, Vila do Porto

Great location next to the ocean combined with fresh food and excellent service. The menu has delicious seafood and meat dishes. The food is great and the prices are very reasonable.

Garrouchada +351 296 883 038
Rua Dr. Luís Bettencourt 25, Vila do Porto

If you are a big meat eater, then this is the place to visit. Great local food with for reasonable prices. Excellent service and also a good place to just have a few drinks at the bar.

Bars and Clubs

Conversation with Letters +351 296 883 415
Vila Do Porto, Portugal

Conversation with Letters is a bar/ cafe located in Vila Do Porto. Cold beers, good coffee and light snacks are available. If you want to watch sports while on the island then this is the place to come.

Bar dos Anjos +351 296 886 734

R. Francisco Lopes Anjo

Bar dos Anjos is a good place to have a few drinks and eat a light meal.The sandwiches and burgers at Bar dos Anjos are excellent.Go outside and enjoy the stunning view from the terrace.

Organizações Central, Pub E Ginásio +351 296 882 513

Rua Doutor Luís Bettencourt, 20, Vila Do Porto,
Ilha De Santa Maria

Fantastic pub with great food and service. This is the kind of place you come to for a few beers and fabulous food. Great pub lunches with a great atmosphere and excellent service.Even if you don't drink beer come here just for the food its outstanding.

Fun Activities on the Island

Go Whale Watching

With 20 different kinds of whales in the Azorean seas, you'd surely have a spectacular time trying to know this species—truly a magical, unforgettable sight to behold.

Praia Formosa

Beaches

Santa Maria definitely has a bevy of beaches that you will most definitely enjoy—and they're white sand beaches at that.Make sure to check out Praia Formosa Beach.Praia Formosa Beach is rated as one of the most beautiful beaches in the Azores.The beach is surrounded by beautiful mountains and the water is clear and warm.

Sao Lorenco

Visit the Santa Maria Gardens

The botanical gardens boast of orchards and old pastures, and is located at the Valley of Flamengos, specifically at the Sao Lorenco Farm—where you'd get to see flora and fauna of every kind.

Check the Santa Maria Mills

One of the oldest mills in Azores, the Santa Maria Windmills have that classic Mediterranean charm in them—and are actually smaller than other European models, with triangular sails and domes that'll surely amaze you.

Try Boating

Santa Maria has beautiful, pristine seas—so it would be a shame not to be able to experience it for what it is. Therefore, boating really should be done, so you not only get to traverse the seas, you might see wondrous dolphins, too—and they'll accompany you to the crossings of the island. Amazing!Contact Golden Sail Azores to take a boat trip around the island.

Golden Sail Azores
   Baixa do Vigário
   Phone: +351 296884277
   Mobile: +351 966302056
   Email: info@goldensailazores.com

Watch the birds

Azores have a lot of bird species that you will be in awe to see—these include the storm petrels, the eagle, and even drakes, amongst others. Watch as the birds take flight and come home to their nests—and just be in awe of them living in such a beautiful natural reserve.

Diving

Santa Maria is a top diving destination and offers great diving experiences for visitors. Mantamaria Dive Center offers different diving experiences around the island. Remember to bring your proof of diving experience or proof of certification to make sure you have the best experience possible with Mantamaria Dive Center. Safety is priority number 1.

Mantamaria Dive Center
Vila do Porto Santa Maria Açores Marina de,Vila do Porto
+351 296 882 166

Jeep Safari

Go on a Jeep Safari around the island. If you go with Bootla Tours, you will have the option of half or full-day safaris. This is a great way to see the island and get all the information from an experienced guide.

Bootla Tours
Lugar da Cruz Teixeira Ilha da ,Santa Maria, Açores,Vila do Porto
+351 963 874 547 / +351 911 849 546
info@bootla.pt

Santa Maria On Foot or By Bike

If you want to experience Santa Maria by foot(trekking) or bike then you have the opportunity with Bootla Tours. You will have the option of choosing from five different walking trails on the island. Contact Bootla Tours for more information.

Bootla Tours
Lugar da Cruz Teixeira Ilha da ,Santa Maria, Açores,Vila do Porto
+351 963 874 547 / +351 911 849 546
info@bootla.pt

12

Terceira

Last but not the least is Terceira, a place where you can enjoy swimming in beaches near the island's beautiful stone walls, see the beautiful colors of the tranquil seas, and enjoy its mystery—as not much is known about it.

Where to Stay

Quinta Dos Figos +351 913 454 302
R. das Pedras 34, Cabo da Praia

This lovely farm stay is only a 10 min drive from the airport. This is a vintage hotel with big rooms and comfortable beds.The beautiful garden and location are what makes this place a great place to stay. The host is very friendly and helpful.

Terceira Mar Hotel +351 295 402 280
Portões de São Pedro, nº 1, Angra do Heroísmo

Terceira Mar is a 4-star hotel overlooking Fanal Bay. This is a fabulous hotel with a salt-water infinity pool and a beautiful big garden. The rooms are modern and soundproof with wifi and cable TV. The view over the ocean just compliments an already excellent hotel.

My Angra Boutique Hostel +351 963 505 087
R. de São Pedro 168, Angra do Heroísmo

My Angra Boutique Hostel is exceptional for a hostel type hotel. Even with shared public spaces like bathrooms, kitchen, and lounge, the hotel is till sparkling clean and comfortable. The place has a warm homely feel to it. Comfortable rooms, great service, and good location. The breakfast is outstanding.

Azores Angra Garden +351 295 206 600
Praça Velha, Angra do Heroísmo

Azores Angra Garden Plaza Hotel is a modern 4-star hotel located in the central square. This is a perfect location for exploring the historic city center. The facilities of the hotel are beautiful and the staff friendly.The facilities include an indoor pool, jacuzzi, and a gym.

Museums/Galleries

<u>Museu do Vinho</u> +351 965 667 324 / +351 295 908 305
Canada do Caldeiro 3, Biscoitos

Located near the whale-watching museum, this place tells you all about the centuries-old industry of wine-making in the Azores. You might even taste amazing wine, and might take some home too.

ı do Angra do Heroismo +351 295 240 800

.eira de São Francisco, Angra do Heroísmo

If you want to learn more about the history of the Azores, make sure that you check this place out as it is dedicated for that.

Angra do Heroismo

Explore Angra do Heroísmo

Angra do Heroísmo is the biggest city on the island of Terceira .The town center is a UNESCO World Heritage site and its a must-see when you come to the island. Take some time and explore the lovely streets of Angra do Heroísmo.

Restaurants

A Canadinha +351 295 216 373
  Av. Infante Dom Henrique 24E, Angra do Heroísmo

It might be a good idea to make a reservation before you come to this popular restaurant. Fresh local food at reasonable prices. Both the meat and seafood dishes are excellent.

Tasca Das Tias +351 295 628 062
  Rua de São João 113,Angra do Heroísmo

This is one of the best traditional Portuguese restaurants on the island. Tasca Das Tias is very popular and again its recommended to make a reservation. The food selection, service, and atmosphere make this a great place to eat.

Cais de Angra +351 295 628 458
  Marina de Angra, Angra do Heroísmo, Angra do Heroísmo

Fantastic location for a restaurant.Beautiful scenery at the harbor with good food and service. The menu has tasty variety, and the prices are reasonable.

Coffee Shops/Cafes

The International Coffee +351 295 700 083
Rua da Palha 50, Angra do Heroísmo

The International Coffee serves excellent coffee, light meals, and desserts. The sandwiches here are outstanding. The staff is friendly, and the cafe has a nice relaxing atmosphere.

Verde Maçã +351 295 218 294
R. Direita 113, Angra do Heroísmo

Verde Maçã is a charming cafe with quality coffee and light meals. The fresh cakes and pastries are outstanding.This cafe is a must-visit while in Terceira.

Bars and Clubs

Havanna Club +351 295 213 192
  Porto das Pipas, 154, Angra do Heroísmo

Havanna Club is a place for a fun night out with friends. You can dance
the night away and enjoy some good beer or cocktails.

Garoupinha Wine Bar +351 295 212 337
  Rua da Garoupinha 8,Angra do Heroísmo

Fun to place to go with a group of friends to drinks some wine enjoy the
evening.One thing to remember that they only sell wine per bottle. So
take some friends and share a bottle or two.

O Pirata +351 295 705 658
  64, R. da Rocha, Angra do Heroísmo

This is a classic Portuguese pub at a great location overlooking the
water. If you enjoy craft beer, good food, and a fantastic atmosphere
then come to O Pirata pub.

Delman Bar & Lounge +351 961 836 423
  Avenida marginal da Praia da Vitoria,Praia da Vitória

You won't find better locations for a bar than this one. This bar is on
the beach and a great place for some cold beer. The bar serves light
meals, and the burgers are excellent.

Fun Activities on the Island

While there, don't forget to do the following:

Beaches

Praia de Angra do Heroísmo

The sandy beaches on the island are Praia de Angra do Heroísmo ,Praia da Vitória and Praia da Riviera.

Natural Swimming Holes

Another good place to swim is the Biscoitos (natural swimming holes).

These natural swimming holes are located on the northern part of the island.

Negrito natural pools are located on the south side of the island. The ocean can get pretty rough here, but it's still a fun place to swim.

Go see Whales and Dolphins.

Don't waste time just visiting Terceira without trying to go dolphin and whale-watching. Ocean Emotion is a company that specializes in whale and dolphin tours around the island. Ocean Emotion has tours that include snorkeling with the dolphins which is a once in a lifetime opportunity. For more information, contact OceanEmotion Azores Whale Watching.

Ocean Emotion Azores
  9700-154 Angra do Heroísmo
  +351 295 098 119
  +351 967 806 964
  oceanemotion.09@gmail.com

Ride horses

It's fun to ride horses in Terceira because of the peaceful, unforgettable trails.

Experiencing the island on horseback is something you will never forget.

Basalto – Clube de Campo is a horse farm that offers guided tours on horseback. The horses are well trained and the whole experience fun and well organised.

Basalto – Clube de Campo
+351 961 016 488
Rua Mártires da Pátria ,Angra do Heroísmo

Try Hiking

Hike in the famous Azores trails and see various flora and fauna that you probably won't see anywhere else. Hike up the famous Santa Bárbara mountain and see the majestic views from the top.But don't forget to take a walk in the Monte Brasil.

Sea Adventures is an adventure company that offers walking tours around the island with a guide showing you the best of the island.

Sea Adventures

Portões de São Pedro n.1,Angra do Heroísmo

+351 927 162 739

Try kayaking and jet-skiing

Terceira has amazing waters—so it would be a shame not to be able to experience it for what it is. Jet skiing and kayaking really should be done, so you not only get to traverse the seas, you might see wondrous dolphins, too—and they'll accompany you to the crossings of the island, and you might have the best photos, too.Contact Sea Adventures for more information.

Sea Adventures

Portões de São Pedro n.1,Angra do Heroísmo

+351 927 162 739

Go Scuba Diving

Discover what Terceira has to offer by checking their amazing scuba-diving sites—all in crystal clear waters that'll help you define what Azores is all about.Contact Octopus Diving Center for more information.

Octopus Diving Center

Avenida Beira Mar, Praia da Vitória

+351 912 513 906

Conclusion

Thank you for reading this book.

Hopefully, with the help of this book, you have learned much about the Azores—and you're now excited for your trip.

Use this guide to make your trip better and more manageable.

Thank you, and enjoy.

Thank You

I want to thank you for reading this book! I sincerely hope that you received value from it!

If you received value from this book, I want to ask you for a favour .Would you be kind enough to leave a review for this book on Amazon?

CPSIA information can be obtained
at www.ICGtesting.com
Printed in the USA
LVHW100158120623
749495LV00026B/363